EMERGING AS THE TOP CANDIDATE FOR THE JOB

"The Job Hunter's Playbook: Strategic Insights for Outshining Competitors in Every Job Application"

BLESS P. WALTON

TABLE OF CONTENTS

CHAPTER 1

UNVEILING THE MODERN JOB LANDSCAPE

In the ever-changing landscape of the modern job market, success in securing the right position requires a deep understanding of its dynamics. This chapter delves into the intricacies of navigating the evolving job market, explores the trends shaping the hiring process, and emphasizes the pivotal role of technology in contemporary job searches.

1.1 Navigating the Evolving Job Market

Gone are the days of a linear career path, where individuals entered a company and spent their entire professional lives climbing the corporate ladder. The job market has evolved into a dynamic ecosystem, influenced by factors such as globalization, technological advancements, and shifting economic landscapes.

Today, job seekers must adapt to a more fluid and interconnected market. The gig economy, remote work opportunities, and project-based employment have become prevalent, offering both flexibility and challenges. Understanding and navigating this evolution is crucial for job hunters aiming to position themselves effectively.

Navigating the evolving job market requires a strategic approach. Job seekers must stay agile, continually updating their skills to align with industry demands. Networking has become more critical than ever, with personal connections often opening doors that traditional applications cannot. This section explores the strategies and mindset needed to thrive in a job market that is in a constant state of flux.

Moreover, the importance of cultivating a personal brand cannot be overstated. In a competitive job market, standing out is essential. Building a strong online presence through platforms like LinkedIn, showcasing expertise, and consistently engaging in professional development activities are all strategies that can set job seekers apart.

1.2 Trends Shaping the Hiring Process

Understanding the current trends in the hiring process is pivotal for job seekers aiming to outshine their competitors. The recruitment landscape is continually evolving, and staying abreast of these trends can provide a competitive edge.

One significant trend is the rise of data-driven recruitment. Companies are increasingly relying on analytics and artificial intelligence to streamline their hiring processes. Job seekers need to be aware of the keywords and skills that automated systems look for and tailor their resumes accordingly. This section delves into the specifics of data-driven recruitment and provides actionable tips for applicants to navigate this aspect effectively.

Another trend shaping the hiring process is the emphasis on cultural fit. Employers recognize the importance of a cohesive and harmonious workplace culture, and candidates who align with these values are often preferred. Job seekers must not only showcase their skills and qualifications but also convey their compatibility with the company culture. Strategies for researching and integrating these cultural aspects into applications and interviews are explored in detail.

Furthermore, remote work has become a significant trend accelerated by global events. Job seekers need to demonstrate their ability to thrive in remote environments, emphasizing their communication skills, self-motivation, and proficiency in relevant technologies. Understanding and addressing this trend can significantly impact a candidate's attractiveness to prospective employers.

1.3 The Role of Technology in Job Searches

Technology has transformed every aspect of our lives, and the job search process is no exception. From online job boards to artificial intelligence-powered recruitment tools, technology plays a central role in connecting employers with potential candidates.

This section explores the various ways technology has revolutionized job searches. Online platforms have become a primary channel for job postings, requiring applicants to adapt their search strategies. Understanding the algorithms behind these platforms, optimizing online profiles, and utilizing niche job boards are all essential components of a successful tech-savvy job search.

Additionally, the advent of applicant tracking systems (ATS) has automated the initial screening process for many employers. Job seekers must tailor their resumes to pass through these systems, ensuring that their applications make it to the next stage. Practical tips for optimizing resumes for ATS and common pitfalls to avoid are discussed in detail.

Moreover, technology has expanded the reach of job seekers through social media. LinkedIn, in particular, has emerged as a powerful tool for professional networking and job searches. This section provides insights into leveraging LinkedIn effectively, from crafting a compelling profile to connecting with industry professionals.

In conclusion, Chapter 1 sets the stage for job seekers by unveiling the complexities of the modern job landscape. Navigating the evolving market, understanding trends shaping the hiring process, and harnessing the power of technology are foundational elements for anyone aspiring to emerge as the top candidate in today's competitive job market.

CHAPTER 2
CRAFTING A WINNING RESUME

In the competitive realm of job hunting, a well-crafted resume is the passport to unlocking career opportunities. This chapter delves into the art of crafting a winning resume, exploring the nuances of building a document that grabs attention, tailoring it for specific roles, and effectively showcasing achievements and skills.

2.1 Building a Resume that Grabs Attention

A resume is often the first point of contact between a job seeker and a potential employer. In a sea of applicants, it is imperative to create a document that not only showcases qualifications but also grabs attention from the get-go.

The opening section of the resume, commonly referred to as the "professional summary" or "career objective," serves as the initial hook. This section should succinctly highlight the candidate's key strengths, skills, and career goals. It is an opportunity to make a memorable first impression, compelling the employer to continue reading.

Beyond the summary, the structure of the resume itself plays a crucial role. A clean, organized layout enhances readability and makes it easier for hiring managers to extract relevant information quickly. This section explores the dos and don'ts of resume formatting, providing practical tips on creating a visually appealing and professional document.

Moreover, incorporating keywords relevant to the industry and position is vital. Many companies use applicant tracking systems (ATS) to screen resumes, and using industry-specific keywords increases the chances of passing through this initial automated phase. Strategies for identifying and strategically placing these keywords are discussed to help job seekers navigate the automated screening process effectively.

Additionally, the inclusion of a skills section allows candidates to highlight key competencies quickly. However, the choice of skills and the way they are presented can significantly impact the impression they create. This section provides insights into selecting and presenting skills in a manner that aligns with the employer's needs and preferences.

2.2 Tailoring Your Resume for Specific Roles

One size does not fit all when it comes to resumes. Tailoring the document for each specific role is a crucial step in the job application process. Generic resumes often get overlooked, as employers seek candidates whose experiences and skills align closely with the requirements of the position.

This section delves into the importance of customization, guiding job seekers through the process of aligning their resumes with the job description. Analyzing the key responsibilities and qualifications outlined in the job posting allows candidates to emphasize the most relevant aspects of their experience.

The "Professional Experience" section is a critical component that should be tailored to highlight accomplishments and responsibilities relevant to the targeted position. Quantifying achievements and using action verbs can add impact, providing concrete evidence of the candidate's contributions in previous roles.

Furthermore, tailoring extends beyond the content of the resume to the language and terminology used. Mirroring the language used in the job description not only demonstrates alignment but also increases the likelihood of passing through ATS, which may be programmed to recognize specific keywords and phrases.

2.3 Showcasing Achievements and Skills Effectively

In a competitive job market, showcasing achievements and skills effectively can be the differentiator that sets a candidate apart from the rest. The "Professional Experience" and "Skills" sections are prime real estate for presenting this information in a compelling manner.

Rather than simply listing job duties, the focus should be on quantifiable achievements. Whether it's exceeding sales targets, streamlining processes, or leading successful projects, highlighting accomplishments provides tangible evidence of the candidate's impact in previous roles.

Using the CAR (Challenge, Action, Result) method is a valuable strategy for presenting achievements. This involves outlining the challenge or problem faced, detailing the actions taken to address it, and concluding with the positive results achieved. This storytelling approach not only provides context but also engages the reader, making the resume more memorable.

The "Skills" section, often a quick reference point for employers, should be crafted thoughtfully. It's not just about listing technical skills but also showcasing transferable skills such as communication, problem-solving, and leadership. Aligning these skills with the specific requirements of the job amplifies their relevance.

Additionally, incorporating relevant certifications and training can enhance the perceived value of the candidate. Employers often look for continuous learning and professional development as indicators of a proactive and adaptable candidate. This section provides guidance on strategically placing certifications to bolster the overall impression.

In conclusion, Chapter 2 underscores the importance of a meticulously crafted resume in the job-hunting process. Building a resume that grabs attention, tailoring it for specific roles, and showcasing achievements and skills effectively are essential steps in positioning oneself as the top candidate in a competitive job market.

CHAPTER 3

MASTERING THE ART OF COVER LETTERS

In the intricate dance of job applications, the cover letter is your chance to step into the spotlight and showcase the person behind the resume. This chapter delves into the art of mastering the cover letter, exploring the power of personalization, strategies for addressing employer needs, and common pitfalls to avoid.

3.1 The Power of Personalized Cover Letters

A cover letter is not merely a formality; it's a personalized introduction to the candidate. Crafting a cover letter that resonates with the hiring manager can make the difference between being overlooked and standing out in a sea of applicants.

The opening paragraph sets the tone, and a generic introduction rarely captures attention. Personalization begins here by addressing the hiring manager by name, if possible, and expressing genuine interest in the position and the company. This section explores the importance of a compelling opening and provides tips for tailoring it to each application.

Beyond personalizing the salutation, the body of the cover letter is an opportunity to connect the dots between the candidate's skills and experiences and the requirements of the job. Rather than reiterating the resume, the focus should be on telling a story that aligns with the company's values and mission. This chapter provides guidance on weaving a narrative that showcases the candidate's unique qualities and contributions.

Moreover, research plays a crucial role in personalization. Understanding the company's culture, recent achievements, and industry trends allows the candidate to demonstrate genuine interest and enthusiasm. Referencing specific aspects of the company in the cover letter adds a layer of authenticity that resonates with hiring managers.

3.2 Strategies for Addressing Employer Needs

A well-crafted cover letter not only introduces the candidate but also addresses the specific needs of the employer.

Understanding what the company is looking for in a candidate and tailoring the cover letter to address those needs is a strategic approach that can significantly impact the hiring decision.

The body of the cover letter should be structured to align the candidate's skills and experiences with the requirements outlined in the job description. Each paragraph can be dedicated to a key aspect of the candidate's qualifications, demonstrating a clear connection to the employer's needs.

Using the language of the job description is a powerful strategy. This not only ensures that the cover letter passes through automated tracking systems but also resonates with the hiring manager. It shows that the candidate understands the key priorities of the role and positions themselves as the ideal solution.

Moreover, quantifying achievements in the cover letter provides tangible evidence of the candidate's capabilities. Whether it's improving efficiency, increasing revenue, or successfully leading a team, using metrics adds credibility and demonstrates the real-world impact of the candidate's contributions.

3.3 Avoiding Common Cover Letter Pitfalls

While a well-crafted cover letter can elevate a job application, common pitfalls can diminish its effectiveness. This section highlights the most prevalent mistakes and offers guidance on how to avoid them, ensuring that the cover letter serves as a powerful asset rather than a hindrance.

One common pitfall is being overly generic. A generic cover letter that could be applied to any job opportunity lacks the personalization and specificity needed to stand out. This chapter provides insights into tailoring each cover letter to the unique requirements of the position and company.

Another pitfall is the repetition of information already present in the resume. The introductory letter ought to supplement the resume, not copy it. Instead of listing qualifications, the focus should be on providing context and telling a compelling story that adds depth to the candidate's profile.

Additionally, overused clichés and generic language can undermine the impact of a cover letter. Phrases like "hardworking," "team player," and "results-driven" are common and don't provide meaningful insights into the candidate's unique qualities. This section explores alternative ways to convey these attributes with specificity and authenticity.

In conclusion, Chapter 3 emphasizes the importance of mastering the art of cover letters in the job application process. The power of personalization, strategies for addressing employer needs, and the avoidance of common pitfalls are all essential elements in creating a cover letter that captures the attention of hiring managers and positions the candidate as the ideal fit for the role.

CHAPTER 4

LEVERAGING ONLINE PRESENCE FOR SUCCESS

In the digital age, a strong online presence is a formidable asset in the job-hunting landscape. This chapter explores the strategic use of online platforms to enhance career prospects. From the professional networking giant LinkedIn to creating a cohesive online brand and harnessing the power of various social media channels, we delve into the nuances of leveraging online presence for success.

4.1 Harnessing the Power of LinkedIn

LinkedIn has evolved from a mere professional networking site to an indispensable tool for job seekers and recruiters alike. Harnessing the full potential of LinkedIn can significantly enhance one's visibility and opportunities in the job market.

A compelling LinkedIn profile starts with a professional and attention-grabbing headline. This is the first thing that potential employers and connections see, and it should succinctly convey the candidate's expertise and aspirations. This section explores the art of crafting a compelling headline that stands out in a crowded digital space.

The profile summary is the candidate's opportunity to tell their professional story. Beyond listing skills and experiences, the summary should provide insight into the candidate's personality, values, and career goals. Including keywords relevant to the candidate's industry and career aspirations can optimize the profile for search algorithms. Moreover, the experience and skills sections should be curated with a strategic approach. Highlighting key achievements and using action verbs in the experience section adds depth to the profile. Endorsements and recommendations from colleagues and supervisors contribute to social proof, validating the candidate's skills and competencies.

Engaging with the LinkedIn community is equally crucial. Actively participating in discussions, sharing industry insights, and connecting with professionals in the field contribute to a dynamic and influential online presence. This section provides guidance on effective networking strategies and etiquette on LinkedIn.

4.2 Creating a Professional Online Brand

Beyond individual platforms like LinkedIn, the concept of a professional online brand encompasses the cohesive representation of an individual's skills, values, and expertise across various online channels. This section explores the steps to create and maintain a consistent professional brand.

The initial step is to lead an individual brand review. This involves assessing existing online profiles, ensuring consistency in information, and identifying areas for improvement. Crafting a unique value proposition and identifying key themes that align with the candidate's career goals contribute to a strong personal brand.

A personal website or blog can be a powerful addition to a professional online brand. It serves as a centralized hub for showcasing accomplishments, sharing insights, and providing a more comprehensive view of the candidate's expertise. This section explores the elements of an effective personal website and strategies for its maintenance.

Visual elements, including a professional headshot and consistent design elements across platforms, contribute to a cohesive brand image. This section provides insights into the importance of visual consistency and tips for creating a visually appealing online presence.

Moreover, the strategic use of keywords across online platforms enhances the discoverability of the candidate. This involves incorporating industry-specific terms and skills into online profiles and content.

Techniques for identifying and strategically using keywords are explored in detail.

4.3 Using Social Media to Your Advantage

While LinkedIn is a dedicated professional networking platform, other social media channels can also play a role in enhancing one's online presence. From Twitter to Instagram, each platform offers unique opportunities for engagement and networking.

Twitter, with its fast-paced and dynamic nature, is an excellent platform for staying updated on industry trends and participating in relevant conversations. Creating and curating content that showcases expertise and thought leadership can attract the attention of industry professionals and potential employers. This section provides strategies for maximizing the impact of Twitter in the job search process.

Instagram, primarily known for visual content, can be leveraged to provide a more personal and behind-the-scenes look at the candidate's professional life. Sharing stories, highlights, and visuals that align with the professional brand contributes to a well-rounded online presence. Tips for maintaining a professional yet authentic Instagram presence are discussed in this section.

However, caution is advised when using personal social media platforms. Employers often explore candidates' public profiles to gain additional insights. This section explores strategies for ensuring that personal social media accounts align with the professional brand and do not hinder career prospects.

In conclusion, Chapter 4 emphasizes the pivotal role of online presence in the modern job market. From harnessing the power of LinkedIn to creating a cohesive professional brand and strategically using various social media channels, job seekers can amplify their visibility and stand out in a crowded digital landscape. A well-crafted online presence not only enhances career opportunities but also contributes to the overall narrative of the candidate's professional journey.

CHAPTER 5
ACING INTERVIEWS AND STANDING OUT

Navigating the interview process is a critical phase in the job-seeking journey. This chapter delves into the strategies for acing interviews, encompassing the preparation for different interview formats, confidently tackling tough questions, and leaving an indelible impression that sets candidates apart.

5.1 Preparing for Different Interview Formats

Interviews come in various formats, each designed to assess different aspects of a candidate's suitability for a role. From traditional face-to-face interviews to virtual and panel interviews, preparing for diverse formats is key to success.

Traditional Face-to-Face Interviews:

- Dressing professionally and arriving early.

- Establishing rapport with the interviewer through a firm handshake and maintaining eye contact.

- Navigating common interview questions and providing concise yet comprehensive answers.

Virtual Interviews:

- Testing technology beforehand to avoid technical glitches.

- Ensuring a professional and well-lit background.

- Maintaining eye contact with the camera to create a sense of connection.
- Managing non-verbal cues effectively in a virtual setting.

Panel Interviews:

- Acknowledging all panel members with eye contact and distributing attention evenly.
- Addressing questions to specific panel members when appropriate.
- Showcasing adaptability and interpersonal skills in a multi-interviewer setting.

Preparation is the cornerstone of success in any interview format. This section explores the importance of researching the company, understanding the job role, and anticipating potential questions. Tailoring responses to highlight relevant experiences and aligning them with the company's values contribute to a strong interview performance.

5.2 Answering Tough Questions with Confidence

Tough questions are an inevitable part of the interview process, designed to assess a candidate's ability to handle challenges and think on their feet. Answering these questions with confidence and poise is essential to leaving a positive impression.

Behavioral Questions:

- Using the STAR method (Situation, Task, Action, Result) to structure responses.

- Providing specific examples from past experiences to illustrate skills and competencies.

- Demonstrating self-awareness and a willingness to learn from challenging situations.

Situational Questions:

- Approaching hypothetical scenarios with a logical and methodical thought process.

- Balancing creativity with practicality in proposing solutions.

- Communicating clearly and concisely, showcasing problem-solving skills.

Curveball Questions:

- Staying composed and maintaining a positive attitude.

- Leveraging these questions as an opportunity to showcase adaptability and creativity.

- Tying responses back to core competencies and the needs of the role.

Confidence in answering tough questions stems from thorough preparation and practice. This section explores the value of mock interviews, seeking feedback, and refining responses to common challenging questions. Developing a mindset that views tough questions as opportunities rather than obstacles is pivotal in conveying resilience and composure.

5.3 Strategies for Leaving a Lasting Impression

Leaving a lasting impression goes beyond providing strong answers to questions. It involves showcasing a genuine enthusiasm for the role, a clear understanding of the company, and a demonstration of one's unique value proposition.

Research and Personalization:

- Demonstrating knowledge of the company's history, values, and recent achievements.

- Tailoring responses to reflect an understanding of the specific challenges and goals of the organization.

- Expressing genuine interest in the role and how it aligns with the candidate's career aspirations.

Asking Thoughtful Questions:

- Engaging the interviewer with well-researched and relevant questions.
- Seeking clarification on the company's expectations and culture.
- Demonstrating a long-term perspective by inquiring about growth opportunities within the organization.

Follow-Up Actions:

- Sending a customized thank-you email in no less than 24 hours of the meeting.
- Reiterating enthusiasm for the role and appreciation for the opportunity.

- Incorporating specific elements from the interview in the follow-up to reinforce memorable points.

Moreover, non-verbal communication plays a significant role in leaving a positive impression. Maintaining good posture, smiling, and exhibiting active listening skills convey professionalism and engagement. This section provides insights into the nuances of non-verbal communication and its impact on the overall impression.

In conclusion, Chapter 5 underscores the importance of excelling in interviews to stand out in the competitive job market. Preparing for different interview formats, confidently answering tough questions, and leaving a lasting impression require a combination of thorough preparation, adaptability, and strategic communication. Acing interviews not only increases the likelihood of securing the job but also contributes to building a positive professional reputation that extends beyond the hiring process.